The Stanmores
In Camera

by Alf Porter

QUOTES LIMITED

MCMXCII

Published by Quotes Limited
Whittlebury, England

Typeset in Plantin by
Key Composition, Northampton, England

Pictures Lithographed by
South Midlands Lithoplates Limited, Luton, England

Printed by Busiprint Limited
Buckingham, England

Bound by Charles Letts Limited
Edinburgh, Scotland

ISBN 0 86023 604 8

Bibliography

Revd B. J. Armstrong. *Some Account of the Parish of Little Stanmore* (Edgware, 1849)

Percy Davenport, *Old Stanmore* (Stanmore 1933)

Charles L. Holness, *St. Lawrence Church, Little Stanmore: A Short Guide* (Harrow 1937)

Royal Commission on Historical Monuments of England: Middlesex (London 1937) pp16-17 and pp114-115

Walter W. Druett, *The Stanmore and Harrow Weald through the Ages* (Hillingdon, 1938)

George Cross, *Suffolk Punch* (April, 1939)

Arthur Mee, ed, *Middlesex* (London 1953)

Nikolaus Pevsner, *The Buildings of England, Middlesex* (Harmondsworth 1951)

Norman G. Brett-James, *Middlesex* (London 1953)

Michael Robbins, *Middlesex* (London 1953)

C. F. Baylis, *A Short History of Edgware and the Stanmores in the Middle Ages* (London 1957)

Friends of St Johns: *A Guide to the Parish Church of Saint John the Evangelist, Great Stanmore* (Stanmore 1965)

Victoria County History: *Middlesex Vol IV* (London, 1971) *Vol V* (London, 1976)

Peter G. Scott, *Harrow and Stanmore Railway* (Greenhill, 1972)

Stephen A. Castle, Excavations in Pear Wood, Brockley Hill, Middlesex, 1948-1973, *Transactions of the London and Middlesex Archaeological Society*, Vol 26 (1975) pp267-277 Roman pottery from Brockley Hill, Middlesex, 1966 and 1972 and 1974, *Transactions of the London and Middlesex Archaeological Society*, Vol 27 (1976) pp206-227

Alan W. Ball, *The Countryside Lies Sleeping* (London 1981)

Joan Johnson, *Excellent Cassandra* (Gloucester, 1981) *Princely Chandos* (Gloucester, 1984)

Alfred E. Porter, *Edgware and the Stanmores in Camera: A Nostalgic Record* (Farnborough, 1984) *Old Edgware in Camera* (Buckingham, 1991)

Introduction

Little Stanmore is a long and narrow parish, stretching from Burnt Oak in the south to Elstree village in the north. Roman Watling Street, the great military highway from Dover to Chester, via London and St Albans, forms its eastern boundary. Towards the north end of the parish and extending into the neighbouring parish of Edgware, is Brockley Hill, where archaeological excavations have disclosed evidence of occupation in the Mesolithic period, c8,500-4,000 BC. Bronze Age worked flints, including an arrowhead, have been recovered. More important, Brockley Hill is thought to be the site of *Sulloniacis*, which was mentioned in the Second Antonine Itinerary as lying 12 Roman miles from *Londinium* (London) and nine from *Verulamium* (St Albans). Excavations from 1937-1975, instead of providing evidence of a posting station or indeed any substantial buildings, have disclosed a flourishing Roman pottery manufacturing centre dating from cAD 50-160. Occupation of a more domestic nature continued into the late 2nd, 3rd and 4th centuries AD.

At Pear Wood, near Brockley Hill, in the Parish of Little Stanmore, there is a linear earthwork which appears to be the 'Grrymesdich' mentioned in documents dating from 1306 and 1535. Archaeological excavations in 1973 recovered 4th century artifacts from the bottom of the north bank of the earthwork. A date some time in the 4th-6th centuries AD is likely.

The Manor of Stanmore was granted by King Offa of Mercia to St Albans Abbey in 793. However, by the reign of Edward the Confessor, 1042-1066, 9½ hides of this land were held by Algar, Earl Harold's man. Little Stanmore was a possession of the Priory of St Bartholomew the Great, Smithfield.

Great and Little Stanmore, the two medieval parishes covered by this book, have left us with memories of some of the great personalities that have graced this part of England.

Canons, in Little Stanmore, an estate held by the Priory during the Middle Ages, had a most distinguished owner from 1713 onwards. He was James Brydges (1673-1744), MP for Hereford, first Duke of Chandos and Paymaster General of forces abroad from 1707-1712. He set about building a magnificent mansion within extensive landscaped grounds, including fine gardens, a lake and avenues. Sadly, this fine country seat was demolished after his death and replaced with a more modest building which survives this day, albeit in an altered form. The contents of Canons were dispersed — the interior of the chapel went to Witley Court, Great Witley, Worcestershire; the organ to Gosport Parish Church, Hampshire and the pews, font etc to Fawley Parish Church, Buckinghamshire. Only the classical Temple, gardens and Parish Church of St Lawrence, Little Stanmore survive, to remind us of the work of the Duke.

Among the great names associated with Great Stanmore was Sir John Wolstenholme (died 1639), who helped to finance the expedition by Henry Hudson and William Baffin to North Canada. Cape Wolstenholme and Wolstenholme Sound are named after him. The ruinous red brick church at Great Stanmore, which has recently been renovated, was built in 1632, at the sole expense of Sir John. It was consecrated by William Laud (1573-1645) when Bishop of London (1628-1633).

The foundation stone of the present Parish Church of St John the Evangelist was laid by George Hamilton Gordon, fourth Earl of Aberdeen (1784-1860) on 14 March, 1849 in the presence of the Dowager Queen Adelaide (1792-1849) — Queen of William IV. George Hamilton Gordon had strong connections with Stanmore, having married the daughter of the Marquess of Abercorn, who resided at Bentley Priory. Gordon's son, the Hon Douglas Gordon, was Rector of Great Stanmore from 1848-1857. George Hamilton Gordon was Prime Minister from 1852-1855 and is buried at Great Stanmore. This was the last public appearance of Queen Adelaide, who was then also living at Bentley Priory.

Stanmore developed as a farming community, early on known as *Stanmera*. Thus it remained until the railways came — steam first, then the Underground Northern Line to Edgware in 1923. When the Bakerloo reached it in the thirties, Stanmore was the 'end of the line' so it was also on the urban perimeter. This made it both popular, and selective; when the line to Elstree was shelved, it was more so.

Post-war Green Belt policy meant the Elstree extension never happened. Then the MI Motorway swept by, opening up the hinterland, while limiting local development. Thus Stanmore has held the line for fifty years; there is no new building land, so new building is limited to increased density of existing sites. Stanmore is now the buffer between town and country — the end of the line.

Acknowledgements are due to Stephen Castle for his help with the text.

Edgware High Street, looking north in 1903-1904; the village lies between two parishes. On the right (east) side is the parish of Edgware and on the left (west) side, the parish of Little Stanmore (Whitchurch). The road to the right is Station Road, on the north of which is the Boot. This Georgian building, once known as the Boot and Spur, was demolished in 1935. The road to the left is Whitchurch Lane, leading to Little Stanmore and on to Great Stanmore.

This drawing by Horace Wright, the local chemist and historian, shows a 16th century timber-framed building on the Little Stanmore side of Edgware High Street. Once an alehouse called the Sawyers Arms, it has survived.

6

A group of ex-servicemen pose after attending a service at the War Memorial, Edgware High Street, early 1920s.

Whitchurch Lane looking west, shows the Old Police Station (left) and Thorndikes the bakers' stables on the right; 1903.

x

Candidate the Hon W. Peel, in a motor car on election day, 22 January 1906, outside the old Whitchurch Institute, Whitchurch Lane, Little Stanmore.

Supporters of the Hon W. Peel stand in a farm cart, outside the old Masons Arms, on the corner of Edgware High Street and Whitchurch Lane, January 1906.

10

In Whitchurch Lane, looking east towards Edgware High Street c1920, the sheep are heading towards Angus Keen's farm, at the end of a trackway that is now Handel Way.

W. E. Highams' tug-'o-war team in 1906 is pulling away where today lies the bottom of Buckingham Road; the white gate on the left leads into Whitchurch Lane.

Whitchurch Lane 1935; Mead Road is just out of the picture on the left, and Buckingham Road on the right.

Buckingham Road and Whitchurch Lane c1935; the picture was taken from the corner of Chandos Crescent.

Whitchurch Lane, Little Stanmore, view to the west c1910; Montgomery Road now runs from the bottom right of the picture.

St Lawrence Parish Church, Whitchurch Lane, Little Stanmore; the low stone tower of c1500 is all that remains of the medieval church. The nave and chancel were rebuilt in brick in 1715 at the expense of James Brydges, first Duke of Chandos, who lived at Canons. The Church is noted for its fine interior paintings by Bellucci, Slater, Laguerre and Verrio, and the wood carvings of Grinling Gibbons. The Chandos Mausoleum houses, among others, a fine monument to James Brydges (1673-1744) and his first two wives. The four wooden graveboards remembered the Stone family, Elizabeth, her son Joseph, husband Samuel, and daughter, Mary.

St Lawrence Parish Church, inside in 1905, showing the magnificent paintings, especially the trompe l'œil painting on the north wall, and the early forms of lighting.

LEFT: St Lawrence Parish Church organ is the one on which George Frederick Handel played while he was staying at Canons. RIGHT: St Lawrence Parish Church before the lych-gate; it was erected in memory of Dr Alexander Findlater DSO and dedicated in March 1934.

A group of Little Stanmore ladies and children wait to leave on an outing from St Lawrence Church in the 1920s. Identifiable people include (back row, third from left) Mrs Porter snr and next to her, Mrs Balaam; (third row, fifth from left) Miss Beatrice Highams, and three along, Mrs Bishop; at the end of the row is Mrs Adams; (standing in front, fifth from the left) Mrs Perry and her sister, Mr Snoxell and next but one, Mrs Davies; four from her is Mrs Stoter; sitting is Alec Mair with George Bishop in the cap and Olive Adams.

The old Rectory of St Lawrence, Whitchurch, a fine, early Victorian building, demolished 1966-1967.

The Lake Almshouses (c1910-1920) were founded before 1693 by Mary Lake, widow of Sir Thomas Lake of Canons but were demolished in 1957. The Parish Hall now occupies the site.

Haymaking at Canons Park Farm, Little Stanmore c1920, reflects the rural Middlesex of those days.

Marsh Lane view to the south in c1910.

Dennis Lane, Great Stanmore in 1935; it was once one of the early trackways running through Stanmore and said to be named after Dionesia Bucaute, a prosperous landowner of the 13th century.

Rose Cottage, Dennis Lane with Goerge Cheshire, gardener, in the 1930s; Oak Lodge Close now occupies the site. His wife was in domestic service with (Sir) Rider Haggard, of She and King Solomon's Mines fame.

59-65, The Broadway, Great Stanmore is one of the few suriving historic buildings in the area. A timber-framed building dating from the 16th century, it was originally 110 feet long; one bay was demolished in 1865, but at 90 feet long, this is still one of the longest jettied buildings in England. Its original function is unclear.

This picture of The Broadway, Great Stanmore, shows the pond and water pump and a rather more leisurely mode of transport than we see today, c1905.

The village water pump and pond dominate The Broadway.

LEFT: R. J. Leversuch, watch and cloch repairer, here c1910 had one of the small shops, RIGHT: where a route 106 'bus is about to ascend Stanmore Hill c1912.

Buckingham Cottage, The Broadway, Great Stanmore, a Georgian brick-fronted house, was later demolished to make way for Buckingham Parade shops.

30

In Church Road, Great Stanmore 1910, the building on the right was the old Queens Head alehouse, now the site of Lloyds Bank. The Victorian building, with the white barge boarding beyond, was Great Stanmore's first telephone exchange.

In this Church Road, Great Stanmore, view to the west in 1910, the telephone exchange is on the right and Bedford's General Store just beyond.

Church Road, Great Stanmore; these timber buildings stood near the old Fountain Public House next to the present Fountain House; c1920.

In Church Road, before a Georgian house with fine Venetian window c1914, Mrs Breckenbridge sits on a chair nursing her cat. Would the cat sleep so soundly with the present traffic noise?

The building on the right in Church Road c1905 is the telephone exchange; to the left is Bedford's General Store and on the left is the garden wall of a large house called The Elms.

The Elms, Church Road, Great Stanmore c1910. Now the site of Elms Tennis Club, this Victorian House was typical of the many large villas in the area and when it was demolished the various components were incorporated into a desirable residence elsewhere in Stanmore, which still stands.

Elm Park, Stanmore, view to the north in 1920.

Church Road, Great Stanmore in 1910; the Fountain pub is on the right and Bedford's general shop is opposite.

Church Road, Great Stanmore, looking west in 1910; a minute of the Vestry meeting on 16 September 1750 states 'Petter Sharp . . . obtained the consent of the parishoners . . . for keeping a Public House at the sign of the Crown'. The Crown Hotel, now replaced, was clearly a building of the 18th century. Here it advertises the London and North Western steam service from Edgware to Finchley.

Church Road, Great Stanmore, looking east in 1915.

The Manor House and gardens looked like this when the estate was laid out in 1930.

Stanmore Railway Station (c1905); it was mainly due to the enthusiasm of Mr Frederick Gordon, as Chairman and majority shareholder, that this railway was built. Opened in December 1890, it served as the terminus of the London and North Western Railway branch line from Harrow to Wealdstone. Frederick was founder and Chairman of Gordon Hotels Ltd, a company that owned several hotels both in England and on the continent. Gordon Avenue was named after him.

Passengers wait on Stanmore Railway Station for the arrival of the first train in December, 1890.

At Stanmore Railway Station platform around 1900, the stationmaster stands on the left. This magnificent country railway station closed in 1964. Only the booking hall complex survives today, as a private residence.

A group of navvies (navigators) gather in front of one of the tents of a camp set up by the Church Army for their use when they built the Stanmore Railway 1889-1890. The site is now occupied by Abercorn Road.

Horse and trap and a flock of sheep occupy Gordon Avenue, Great Stanmore in 1920.

A Fowler 2-6-2 tank engine 40048 with a passenger train leaves Stanmore Village Station c1950 — the sign is a fond memory.

Old Church Lane, Great Stanmore c1920 continues to the left, Belmont Lane to the right and Abercorn Road now runs through the fields beyond — here advertising 'Ideal Homes'.

In Old Church Lane, Great Stanmore, this was the view to the north in 1920.

Church Corner, Great Stanmore c1914; the wooden fence on the left surrounds the churchyard, Green Lane runs to the right and the horse and water cart are filling up before proceeding west along Uxbridge Road.

The foundation stone of the present Church of St John the Evangelist, Great Stanmore was laid on 14 March 1849, by the Right Hon the Earl of Aberdeen, in the presence of the Dowager Queen Adelaide. George Hamilton Gordon, fourth Earl of Aberdeen, had married the daughter of the Marquess of Abercorn, and his son, the Hon Douglas Gordon, was Rector at the time.

In this view to the south-east c1930 the bungalow (left) is Hollond Lodge, built by Mrs Ellen Hollond in memory of her husband, Mr Robert Hollond of Stanmore Hall.

Inside the Parish Church of St John the Evangelist, Great Stanmore (1930) the font on the right was given by Queen Adelaide.

LEFT: The shrine outside St John's Parish Church is dedicated to those men of Great Stanmore who died in the Great War of 1914-1919. RIGHT: The Burnell monument in St John's Parish Church; John Burnell, who died in 1605, was a merchant of the City of London and a Freeman of the Worshipful Company of Clothworkers. Barbara Burnell, his wife, survived him by some twenty years and was Lady of the Manor.

The ruinous Parish Church of St John the Evangelist, Great Stanmore (1903-1905) was consecrated by William Laud, when Bishop of London, in 1632. The entry in Laud's diary for 17 July, 1632 reads: 'I consecrated the Church at Stanmore Magna, built by Sir John Walstenham'. Sir John (Wolstenholme) paid for the Church. An earlier parish church, dedicated to St Mary and of medieval date, was in Old Church Lane.

The Old Rectory, Great Stanmore (c1920) was a red brick edifice dating from 1730. The timber used in its construction was given by James Brydges, the first Duke of Chandos. It was demolished in the 1950s.

St John's Parish Church handbell ringers c1915 included (seated in the centre) Mr E. J. Leversuch, for many years their captain.

Stanmore Park, Great Stanmore in the 1920s was a graceful 18th century mansion demolished in 1938, and was home at various times to the Drummond family (founders of Drummonds Bank), Lady Aylesford and Lord Castlereagh.

The drawing room at Stanmore Park.

This trackway led to Park Farm, which was the Home Farm for Stanmore Park. It is now a road called The Chase, leading from Uxbridge Road to Gordon Avenue.

Three omnibuses belonging to the London General Omnibus Company stand outside the Seven Balls at Harrow Weald in 1912. This fine timber-framed building dates from the 17th century or earlier.

At the bottom of Stanmore Hill, this was the view to the north in 1903. The Queens Head is on the left. The Vestry minutes of 4 November 1756 mentions 'a vestry holden in the Vestry room in the Church and afterwards adjourned to the Queens Head by reason of the cold weather'. The site is now occupied by Lloyds Bank.

The bottom of Stanmore Hill in 1920 is marked by the London and South Western Bank.

Peace Day celebrations were held in the Recreation Ground c1920.

Stanmore School Group, Standards VI and VII, pose for posterity around 1915.

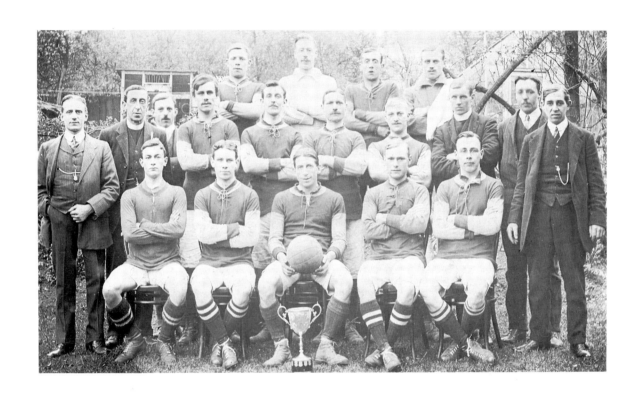

Stanmore Athletic Football Club were winners of the Wembley and Harrow League, Division 2, in 1912-1913.

This was the Post Office and Berwick and Son's Store, Stanmore Hill, in 1920.

The Abercorn Royal Hotel, Stanmore Hill between 1905-1910, a handsome red brick 18th century building with later additions was the scene of a meeting on 21 April 1814, between Louis XVIII of France and the Prince Regent (later George IV). Louis had been in exile at Hartwell near Aylesbury and was on his way to reclaim the throne of France.

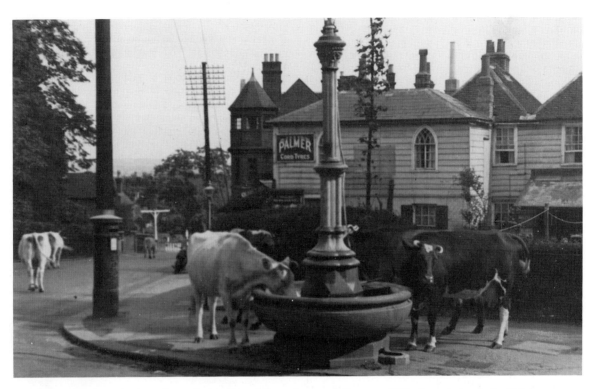

Cows drink from the fountain on the junction of Green Lane and Stanmore Hill, the main bowl of which is now outside St John's Parish Church; it was given by Agnes Keyser, sister of Charles Keyser, who lived at Warren House, Wood Lane.

The Spring Pond, Little Common, Great Stanmore c1912 displayed a delightful mixture of architecture, in what is still one of the few remaining unspoilt parts of Stanmore.

Here is the old water pump in 1930 at Little Common.

ABOVE: Stanmore Hall is a Gothic masterpiece built for John Rhodes in 1847. It was later acquired by Mr Robert Hollond MP, a noted balloonist who, in 1836, travelled by balloon from Vauxhall Gardens, London to Weilberg in Southern Germany — 500 miles in 18 hours. The next owner, William Knox D'Arcy, greatly enlarged the property in 1895, among whose staff OPPOSITE: was the author's mother, Mrs Ellen Porter (née Weatherly), the lady on the right of the front row, c1903.

King Edward VII leaves Warren House, Great Stanmore, after one of his many visits to his great friend, Mr Charles Keyser on 2 June 1907. As Chairman of the Colne Valley Water Company, he was instrumental in supplying piped water to the area.

A cricket match at Stanmore Common in 1853.

Stanmore Cricket Club in 1890.

A group of wounded servicemen and associates gather in front of the Stanmore Cricket Club pavilion during the Great War.

Green Lane, Stanmore, looking south in 1910.

A group of Stanmore residents pose in the late 1940s before an outing (probably) organised by the British Legion. Among the old Stanmore names in the group are: Cheshire, Ebsworth, Fensom, Goddard, Harrowell, Knight, Sweetman, Weatherley and Webb.

Index to Illustrations